ANCHOR
BOOKS

# *JUST ANOTHER DAY*

Edited by

Heather Killingray

First published in Great Britain in 1997 by
ANCHOR BOOKS
1-2 Wainman Road, Woodston,
Peterborough, PE2 7BU
Telephone  (01733) 230761

HB ISBN 1 85930 568 7
SB ISBN 1 85930 563 6

# FOREWORD

Anchor Books is a small press, established in 1992, with the aim of promoting readable poetry to as wide an audience as possible.

We hope to establish an outlet for writers of poetry who may have struggled to see their work in print.

The poems presented here have been selected from many entries. Editing proved to be a difficult task and as the Editor, the final selection was mine.

Poets from all walks of life have gathered to contribute to this book which helps celebrate *Just Another Day.*

This anthology covers every aspect of life from love of a home town, the past, to family life and friends. If you have an appreciation of the many aspects that life offers then this is the book for you.

I trust this selection will delight and please the authors and all those who enjoy reading poetry.

Heather Killingray
Editor

# CONTENTS

# To Margaret

When cold mid-life approaches
And love has not appeared
The heart plans its researches
To calm thoughts that are feared.

But providence can lend a hand,
And did so too, for me,
An opening to a happier land
From my dear bride to be.

Her widowed eyes just bared my breast,
Her offspring graced a charm,
A child of beauty, heaven blessed
Before me to protect from harm.

Child looked at me - her destiny;
Her parent, not her choice,
For blood may claim the pedigree
But love supplants the voice.

My bride, her mother, shared her mood;
Child grew through time and caring,
And gave us pride in parenthood
With joy and sorrow sharing.

Life's winter has displayed its bite
And pruned the family tree.
This elder branch is hanging tight
Now child takes care of me.

*Arch Lang*

## DOLPHINS SMILE

Smiling through an ocean's moods
Torpedo down to depths below.
Piercing through a crystal ceiling
Acrobatic aerial show.

Oh to love life like a dolphin.
Friends of the earth, no enemies made.
But as more are caught in nets illegal
The dolphin's smile begins to fade.

*Patrick Humble*

## PARADISE ISLAND

In the middle of an ocean
600 miles from land
Lies an island called Bermuda
With beautiful pink sand

Nestling in the Gulf Stream
This island in the sun
Is a paradise beyond compare
Where they welcome everyone

Its people are so friendly
Its climate is a pleasure
With an abundance of hibiscus flowers
Which seem to grow forever

I've been there in a hurricane
I've been there in the rain
I've been there in a heatwave
And I love it just the same

Surrounded by deep coral seas
'Neath a sky of azure blue
There's nowhere else I'd rather be
As long as I'm with you

*Decima Watkins*

# A Light For The Soul

The yew berry red and the mistletoe white
Both light the soul's corners on this special night
Reflecting the shimmer of one bright star's rays
Swimming and gliding in the midnight blue haze.

The babe's straw crib bathed in his Father's gold light
Attracts kings and shepherds throughout the long night.
From this day forward, through ages to come
We'll rejoice at Christmas thanking God for His Son.

*Paddy Jupp*

## THE COLD RIPPED MY FORM

The cold ripped my form
You kept me warm
I cried all night
You helped me fight
I fell on the floor
You hugged me more
I found my mother
I found a friend
I found a beginning in the end
I fell in the pit
And death faced me
But there was your hand
That reached for me
And set me free.

*Daniel Witchell*

## CALL UPON MOTHER

When I need someone for my burden to share
>Then I call upon my mother
To make life's highway a little easier to bear
When I need someone to share my hopes and dreams
>Then I call upon my mother
Whose radiant smile conveys what true spirit means
When I need someone for this life to understand
>Then I call upon my mother
Whose feet always stood firm on her own ground
When I need someone for what in life I cannot change
>Then I call upon my mother
Who through difficult times kept within her range
When I need someone for my inner self to believe
>Then I call upon my mother
Whose strong firing heart no-one could deceive
When I need someone to answer who, what and why
>Then I call upon my mother
Whose shining faith would burn out any feeble lie
>When life falls cold and empty
>And her footsteps are no longer there
>Then I call deep into my soul and heart
>To awake the long lost dream
>To become realisation
>For with you and the world
>>Will I truly share.

***Phyllis Blue***

## I'M STILL AROUND

Don't shed any tears believing I've gone,
A quick thought will do - then please hurry on.
Hurry on to life while still there is time
For there's chasms to bridge - horizons to climb.
And all that's precious that we held so dear
Is no less precious because I'm not here.
Other aspirations, no doubt, will entice and tempt -
But please keep just a little of the dreams that we dreamt.

Don't be sad that for me the sun rises no more -
Perhaps I merely journey beyond places you know.
Yet I'll caress your dimpled cheek with every southerly breeze -
Be the March rosebud you kiss in the loneliest of leas.
And every day that you stride through this earth that I leave
I'll be there stride for stride, close, brushing your sleeve.
And at night I'll listen when you need someone to hear -
Kiss your tears, be your strength, your comforter ever near.

So don't shed any tears now that I've gone.
While you breathe for us both I simply go on.
Don't cry at my lowering into the ground -
It's not really me, my darling, I'm still around.

*Malcolm Burrows*

## THE MECCA LOCARNO - LEEDS

We caught the tram, bus, all the same to take us to our pleasure dome
just off Vicar Lane.
We'd dash home from work, grab a bath and a bite to eat
even sometimes missin' egg 'n' chips a favourite treat!
Skin-tight dresses and stiletto heels a-clickin'
Boys were doing the same, hair cut like Elvis, greased back a-slickin'.
Laughing full of zest for life we went there young hearts racin'
Girls always late for a date, spotty youths trying to look 'big'
with a fag hanging from immature lips waitin', pacin'.
Girls with bouffant hair backcombed, lipstick, which to choose?
Lads in tailored suits made by a friend of Uncle Solly,
Complete with winkle-picker shoes if it rained they'd shun a brolly!
We could hear the music as we dashed inside,
excitement we didn't hide.
The friendly DJ in his smart black DJ coaxed us to 'Come on you
guys and gals!' We liked him we felt we were pals?
The Larry Cassidy Quartet played 'Mr Sandman'.
A smoochie - time to cuddle!
Sultry Turks from Leeds University held us too close!
Our hormones in a complete muddle!
We forgot the mill, the factory and the boring office job as we
                                                    canoodled.
We watched Miss Ryan in her tight frocks sing with Edmundo Ross,
                                                    we drooled.
The huge mirrored globe twirled as my young heart whirled,
the clock ticking too fast, the man in the DJ smiled 'Time to go
young lady, it's half past!'
He had ordered me to go! Was it a plan?
Was he in cahoots with my mam?
This was part of growing up, falling in love, getting wed, having
                                                    babies.
Forget the swooning to Al Martino, wash nappies, no maybe's!

The Mecca Locarno Leeds sowed many wondrous seeds,
Who was the man in the smart DJ who changed the lives of us 'guys
'n' gals?
Who called his beloved mum 'duchess', who never told me lies,
who made us feel that we were important, pals.
In those halcyon days he was just 'Jimmy' to you and me,
He's still the same nice guy, but nowadays he's known as . . .
Sir James Saville OBE!

*J M Hefti-Whitney*

## Changing Clouds

Looking out of my window.
Staring into space.
Watching the clouds,
drift along.
Forming different shapes.
I see men, women and children,
With a happy smiling face.
There are mountains,
Palm trees, and even pale blue lakes.
A walrus, and seals, even an
elephant's shape.
Now I see a Cavalier,
White shirt, with frills of lace.
And, an old Victorian gentleman
with a stern look on his face.
It's made me deeply wonder,
Are all those images in space?
Or is it my imagination, for I'd
dearly love to paint?
And if I were an artist
Out of the clouds I'd paint
My pictures would be more
beautiful
Than anyone could ever paint.

*Doreen Petherick Cox*

## GENERATIONS

Drafted, early, to the wars;
The enemy? That of all youth:
Parents, customs, morals, bars:
I struggled, strained, fought nail and tooth

And they fought back. Still tried to damp,
Year after year, the dangerous spark.
To what avail? In each camp
Victory a question mark.

Strange, that now, long afterwards,
We would, I think, mostly agree,
My words being sifted through their words,
Transfigured, magically.

*Peter J Rist*

## FOOD FOR THOUGHT

Like chocolate,
You are hard to resist.

Like sunlit-topped mashed potato clouds,
Blown, early September evenings,
On a cushion of warm aromatic winds
Of your garlic mushroom breath,
You are hard to resist.

You give me food for thought
And more besides.
Life has never been so sweet.

I hunger for you
And how.

Like chocolate,
I want you
Now.

*John Gordon*

## RAINBOW

A rainbow in the sky
So far away so high
Where sun and rain do meet
And one another greet
To form a dazzling bow
Where all the colours glow
At the end a pot of gold
Many people would love to hold
Seven colours we can see
Reaching down to you and me
Red is the colour of a rose
Men give flowers to propose
Orange is a sunset
Where night and day have met
Yellow is a daffodil
Standing on a windowsill
Green is the countryside
Where things grow in their pride
Blue is the sky
Where birds are free to fly
Violet and indigo
Complete the colours of the bow.

*Norman Langdon*

# THE BEAT GENERATION

Tonight the streets pump enthusiasm
This night the clouds won't sleep
Tonight, its people are vibrating
In the air throbs a deep sub beat.

This dawn the masses gather
This race the gods select
The birth of the beat generation
The mother tongue, a strange dialect.

Now their voices are raging
Their drums beat no peace
Come gather the beat generation
The old and stagnant cease.

Now the shaman can rejoice
No guilt of wasting the dawn
Go forward the beat generation
Because for you the earth was born.

**G Brandon**

## SKOMER PUFFINS

Watching the puffins drift alone,
Waves calmly float to seashore,
Sparkles quietly trickle away,
Puffins glide in the sky,
Sea wind blows in their face,
The orangey-red sun goes down,
Puffins flutter to their nest,
As the sun crouches down,
Everything becomes silent.

*Lauren Peach  (10)*

# MRS SMITH AND THE CAROL SINGER

It was Christmas Eve around six o'clock, a perfect Christmas Eve
                                                    kind of night
A million stars twinkled from the sky, snow lay crisp and white
In a quiet street a young boy sang loudly and slightly off-key
'In the Bleak Mid Winter' to the occupant at number three.

After just one verse he rang the bell and said as Mrs Smith answered
                                                    the door
'I know the other verses too missus, I'll sing them, there's only
                                                    three more'
'All right if you must dear' Mrs Smith replied, a broad smile
                                                    lighting her face
'You carry on - I shall be listening, I'll just pop and fetch my purse'

'I'm sorry my dear' said the old lady when she returned to
                                                    the hall
'I have only this bar of chocolate I'm afraid - for I have no change
                                                    at all -
Not a penny have I in my purse - not till next pension day'
'Oh that's all right missus' grinned the likeable urchin, 'I like
                                                    chocolate anyway'

'Merry Christmas then dear' smiled Mrs Smith, before slowly
                                                    closing the door
'Merry Christmas and thanks' called the young tearaway, vaulting
                                                    the wall to number four
It was an hour later or thereabouts, the bell rang again at number three
'Oh no, not another carol singer' sighed Mrs Smith gently lifting the
                                                    cat from her knee

'It's just me again missus - and I've not come to sing' laughed the
                                                    mischievous boy
'But I've done quite well with my carol singing, here's a few coins
                                                    for you too
It might keep you going till pension day, I'm sorry I can't give you
                                                    the lot
But I've not bought Mam's Christmas box yet. I'm just off to get it now
                                                    from the corner shop'

He thrust some coins into Mrs Smith's hand, then sprinted away
                                                          down the street
Church bells rang out the message of Christmas, breaking the silence
                                                          of the night
'Oh yes it was Christmas, indeed it was Christmas' smiled Mrs
                                        Smith as she watched from the door
There running down the street was the very meaning of Christmas -
                  no way could she have said 'Son - I'm not at all poor'

For just like the boy in the carol he sang, the poor boy with no
                                                          gift to impart
The young carol singer to the occupant at number three had simply
                                                          given his heart.

***Frances Doreen Rhodes***

# PRIDE MUST ABIDE

To the hairdresser I must go
even though I hate it so
to suffer the wet and the awful cold 'slosh' (neutraliser)
but what option have I got?
It must be a perm
for mine is at the end of its term,
I sat in the black and chrome chair and waited there
so many mirrors - reflections everywhere

Then the young lady came
a nice girl - Clare was her name!
'No, I don't want it cutting' I said,
'it upsets me to see it on the floor all shed,
mine doesn't grow very much you see -
so I try to 'stretch' it, for around my ears I like it to be!'
Washing and curling - then the dreaded 'cold slosh'
then drying and combing - now I look posh!

After two hours and two cups of tea
I was ready to leave it seemed to me,
Now, there is something I have forgotten - what can it be?
Oh yes, of course, I have to pay - silly me!

*Edna Parrington*

## THE FRONT MAN

Standing in front of the crowd
everyone looking at me
The deadly silence of the room is this my doom?
A sea of faces all waiting to see
'Are they good?' 'Will they be?'
All these questions
I can see, I can feel, I can sense
as a hundred or more people all condense.
In a room full to the brim
things are looking grim.
What if they do not like what they hear
and disperse and disappear
and I'm the only one standing here
The fear is gripping me now
I feel the edge
so sharp and yet blunt
as I stand up before them
right here at the front.
A smile from a friend helps break the ice
A feeling inside
so strong and so nice
helps turn my thoughts
to what lies ahead
as I approach the mike I raise my head
then reach out my hand for the rest of the band
no need to turn around as they all understand.
The music starts
and the silence breaks
and I tell myself *'Yes'*
we've got what it takes.

*Colin Tootell*

## JUST YOU, THE BIKE, AND ME

Off we go to the great outdoors
whether countryside or seaside shores
So lock the door and let us go
I know not where - have no wish to know

Let's get away from the maddening crowd
from the hustle and bustle of life
Let's escape to the great outdoors
away from trouble and strife

Others may have their plush hotels
their comforts and a G & T
But give me a bike, a tent and a pint
And that's the life for me

And when the stars light up the sky
and others are tucked up in bed
we'll sit together you and I
and see the moon and stars overhead

So, open that throttle,
Give it lots of bottle
Let's ride and ride and be free
Just you, the bike and me.

*Jenny Brownjohn*

## NEW LIFE

Have you ever stood in a cornfield
In August, high summer, and heard
The whisper of wheat ears blowing
Softly talking without ever a word.

Have you ever smelled the honeysuckle
On a warm and moonlit night
And wandered alone in the garden
Whilst each bloom was bathed in white light.

Have you ever sat by a river
Hazy and warm in the sun
And watched the dragonflies darting
Peacock blue and green, a dazzle of fun.

Have you ever lazed by the ocean
As the waves curl up on the shore
And breathed in the air, salty tasting
As you fling back your head, wanting more.

Have you ever lost a dear loved one
Known loneliness, too great to bear
Yet nature is there to console you
With moonbeams and stars in her hair.

Enjoy every moment of living
There is so much to wonder at still
Take nothing for granted, but savour
This new life you have started to fill.

*Gwen Norman*

## PENRITH CUMBERLAND

From high on the hill I look down;
There below me lies our town.
This town called Penrith is my home;
From this lovely place I will not roam.

It gives me pleasure and delight
To see it from this great height,
Looking down on the houses and streets
Where people walk and they meet.

The castle and station catch my eye
As through the station a train goes by.
I watch the train travelling so fast,
Then on the fells my eyes are cast.

Away in the distance these fells lie;
They seem to reach up to the sky,
And as the sun beams down on them,
These lakeland mountains are a gem.

As I sit and watch over our town
I think of the good times which abound.
We'll stay here in this town until we die;
We love this place, my wife and I.

*Francis Allen*

## FADING MEMORIES

*(For the ones who filled our lives and broke our hearts)*

Time stretches before me, holding many surprises waiting
                                          to be revealed.
And your stillness brings forth one more revelation which
reminds me that no-one is infinite.
Is it darkness where you are now?
Or are you standing with other providers of the same sadness.
Looking upon us with envious eyes as we venture into the territory
which you can never travel to.
Pain and sadness surround me as your existence fades into a
                                          distant memory.
Yet I try to hold onto it as a comfort from the sight of your demise,
which is still projected into the back of my mind with the
                                          clarity of crystal.
Now I know that I have been blessed in life.
For although you have crossed over into the realms of imagination,
I knew you once.
And for that I am thankful.
Here's to fading memories.

*M E Derbyshire*

## MY SECRET COVE

Exotic places I have seen, I've loved, but left behind,
Then sometimes in a quiet mood, perchance they've come to mind,
But in my heart there's only one so specially loved by me,
And that I call my very own, my cove down by the sea.

To sit there in its shadows cool, so quiet this tranquil scene,
And let trickle through my fingers, the golden sand, washed clean,
To look at lovely weed and shells left by the ebbing tide,
And wonder at this mighty sea and the treasures she must hide.

To watch each little fishing boat slip quietly from the quay,
Then see them pit their craft and strength against this open sea,
So proud they'll be when they return, their catch safe in the hold,
Lobsters, crabs and mackerel, and stories to be told.

Then spray will wash my secret cove and I'll back away from sight,
And tremble at the power she shows though filled with sheer delight,
Exotic places I can see as round the world I rove,
But none this quiet tranquillity found in my secret cove.

*Katie Hill*

## MAN OF STONE

The statue stands
In the middle of the square
Open to the elements
Of the fresh air
Rain to soak it
Sun to erode it
Snow to freeze it
Lightning to strike it
The statue stands
As people walk by
Do not notice it
As they trundle past
The man of stone
Sees everyone
Everything
But never blinks an eye
No tears to run down the cheek
No reasons to cry
It stands up high
Away from it all
Untouched by anyone
Or anything at all
It has no emotion
Or none we can see
What purpose has it?
What reason is there
For the statue to stand?
One day in the future
It will be crushed to sand.

*Martin A Parratt*

## THE EXAM

We all huddle in, one by one,
Like rats in a lab; we're not having fun.
We sit in our places; biting our nails,
Here comes the paper; we all think we'll fail.
Now the clock starts; a minute's gone by,
The girl next to me has started to cry.
Five minutes more; my pen's turned to wood,
If I don't pass; I'll be finished for good.
Ten minutes later; I look at the clock,
This paper's a nightmare; much worse than the mock.
Suddenly my pen's alive,
Ten minutes to go; I'll do it in five.
I'm on the last question; time's running out;
I'm going to die; there is no doubt.
I've finished now; ten seconds to go;
There's still people writing; boy are they slow!
Everyone thinks they've done just fine,
The paper is over; until the *next time!*

*Marie Quelch*

## NIGHTMARE

The sun sinks below
a red stained horizon
as the light of day
falters and dies
and all the creatures
of the night awake

As earth spins
upon its passage through
the toxic clouds which poison
our sad polluted planet
I sink into
a nightmare web of sleep.

In my horrific dream
the black serpent of the night
enfolds its anaconda coils about me
so that its hostile scales
will crush and compress me
into a mindless entity.

In the uncertain hour
before the dawn I wake up
and the nightmare abandons me
then I am free
as the birds' dawn chorus
greets the victorious sun

And we receive
the blessings
of the solar light.

*Stephen Gyles*

## FOUR LEAF CLOVER

I found a four leaf clover
And ran to show my father.

I ran through nettles,
Thorns snagging my skirt.

I ran through valleys,
Broken glass cutting my feet

And ran through alleyways
That twisted and turned

And ran into darkness
Where witches lived with
Emerald eyes and
Wolves opened their snouts
To gobble me up

But I just shut my eyes
And ran, and ran

Until I found him
Washing his car.

Here it is! I opened
My palm but the
Four leaf clover
Had flown away
To somebody else's home -

'Cos the very next day
I watched my father
Get into his car
And drive away.

*Sally Balfe*

# SINCE THAT DAY

You don't even know who I am
And even less what I want
But don't be scared, do not fear
Too sweet and tender is just what I feel.
You'll wonder why
And above all, why me?
So I'll tell you that you're all I see
And that I'm too silly and shy
Besides so many reasons . . .
Although we've just met once.
The foolish things I've done
Since that day when I was doomed
Since that day when I first saw you
And then I never knew what to do
I wish I could take you out of my mind
As you'll never be mine.

***Vicente Matoses Lopez***

## UNTITLED

The storm rages and the thunderbolt strikes down,
Right into the heart of a sleepy market town.
The rain batters a worn footpath,
It tickles the leaves and makes them laugh.
A cat shelters under a thick privet hedge,
As raindrops commit suicide off a rotten window ledge
White faces pressed against cold windowpanes in awe of the storm,
Jump back as another flash lights up the shiny lawn.
Babies scream and young animals cower,
Unaccustomed to the deep rumblings and heavy shower,
The shower begins to slow down,
And the storm rolls off to another town.
When quiet is restored and there is no more thunder,
The quilt is pulled up under the chin and it's back to slumber.

*J P MacMurphey*

## A CUP OF TEA

Where would we be
Without a cup of tea?
Early morning kettles,
Are switched on.
So refreshing, so relaxing,
As one drinks, 'A cup of tea'.
Whether it be, hot or cold
This quenches our thirst,
Revives you -
To face the world -
Of conflict and strife
All the consequences
Of life.
A cup of tea, with friends
Makes the conversation flow,
Putting the world to rights
If only this could be so.
A joke, a laugh, and talk
Gives happiness, companionship, and joy.
How we do, give thanks
*For a cup of tea.*

**Gladys Davenport**

## GRANDAD

They say I am stubborn and set in my ways
they tell me to open my mind;
They laugh at my cap, but then everyone says
you have to be cruel to be kind.

They say I'm dogmatic and way out of touch
they tell me I should 'Get a life';
I have all I need, though it doesn't seem much
just a bed and a shed and a wife.

They turn up their noses if I have a smoke
and call me a social disgrace
I simply ignore all these meddlesome folk
who dictate to the whole human race.

They think that it's odd that I don't have a car
that I choose to walk everywhere;
I try to explain, I don't go very far
so why should I pay to get there.

I'm soft in the head for preferring a book
to watching that tripe on TV;
what they don't realise, if you just use your eyes
you end up with a brain like a pea.

My granddaughter thinks I'm a clever old thing
who knows all there is to be known;
says I can do magic with paper and string
from her there's no high moral tone.

So I'll carry on just the way I have done,
content in my old fashioned ways;
I've seen enough change in the way things are done;
to last me the rest of my days.

*Bob Wydell*

# LE TROISIÈME ÂGE

Awake at six for radio's 'Farming Today'
Grandpa looks out at friesians browsing grass.
Across the bay an oil tanker ploughs its sea-way,
Clear summer day promised by his weather-glass.

Breakfast at seven, bacon, eggs, medication;
Oldster and collie leave the busy kitchen.
Walking to woodlands, icon of contemplation,
Not a robot, but thinking deeply within.

Each day the old farmer knows where he is going,
Through fields rich in sand, clay, humus-making loam.
His toil of ploughing, reaping what he'd been sowing,
Attains life's glory and nature's harvest home.

Despite bifocals, hearing aids and walking stick,
He journeyed on rough tracks with fidelity.
His brain is slower but wiser and cathartic;
Sages find fulfilment with integrity.

One thing is sure, dotage has a hunger for truth.
Beyond poverty, greed, hate, pain, destruction,
Clear vision is goodness, beauty, trust, Nazareth;
Using small tools for large task's completion.

Life's variety endows age with mercy's gifts,
Providence gives strength, from selfish ways release.
Hope signals liberation, from dark fear uplifts;
Elders wake forever in bright clime of peace.

Clear of all gloom and blackout, dawns the Easter light;
Pain and loss are restored in love's endless reign.
Frightened folk rise from the depths to joy's lofty heights;
Rejoice! Creation's course ever shall remain.

*James Leonard Clough*

## When I Was A Child

We walked through deep fields,
Of golden corn.
We looked up you could hardly see,
Where we were going.
We kept on the worn-out path.
In the distant, the church steeple stands tall.
We were going to visit my gran,
She lay in the graveyard.
Fifty year on, my mum and dad
Lay at rest.
It's still as peaceful,
As when I was a child.

*Jean Rickwood*

## OFF TO SCHOOL

When starting at school you feel glum.
It's hard to face life without Mum.
They make you do sports,
Send termly reports
And you long for vacations to come.

*Paul Rand*

## MANCHESTER

Manchester is magic,
Manchester is exciting.
Manchester has music,
Here everything is happening.

It has the snappiest dressers in Britain,
It is the most fashion conscious city.
It has clubs, football and music,
Truly an international city.

What a swinging city it is,
I do not feel a stranger any more.
What a mixture of culture it has,
Chinese, Asians and Africans for sure.

*Dr R Qureshi*

# WITH THE COUNCIL

With the council you work hard every day
With the council you work for little pay
With shovel and picks we dig all day long
With barrows and shovels we move the dirt away
With bars and picks we lift the flags
With hammer and chisels we make the flags fit
With rakes and shovels and barrows we lay the tarmac down
With whackers and road rollers we make the roads and paths flat
With rods we clear the sewers and drains
With jetting we keep them clean
With brushes we clean all up
With wagons we move from place to place
With bin wagons we take your muck
With road sweepers we clean up the dog muck
With wagons we take your old furniture away
With bulldozers we fill the tip in with your rubbish
With paint we put the road markings down
With a few men we put your street lighting up
With the gritter wagon we salt your roads
With shovels and salt we clear the snow
With our hands we build dry-stone-walls
With the council you will have arthritis by 25
With the council you will have to retire before you are 45
With the council most people die before they're 65
With help from God you might live a little time more
With the council, with the council, with the council.

*Donald Jay*

## THE TALL GRASS

The lady with the large brown eyes
waited behind her tortoiseshell glasses.
She had come to be admired.
He in the guise of Adonis also waited.
They stood beside the tall grass,
neither acknowledging the other,
both sated by their own appearance.
Those who passed by thought how lovely
was the tall grass.

Exquisitely poised, the tiger deceives its prey.
Moving without motion amongst the tall grass
that sways with the rhythm of its pulse.
Equally less gainly, the coy wildebeest grazes,
undisturbed and lazy about its obviousness.
Neither acknowledge the cruelty of nature,
both about to enact its most grotesque feature.
Those who passed by thought how lovely
was the tall grass.

*Jon Farmer*

## FRIENDS

Old friends, new friends, they all come and go.
Time goes by sometimes quickly sometimes slow.
And all in all, we should keep on the ball
What ever the weather, be it wet or fine
Keep the washing clean and all on the line.

*Alberta Usher*

## POLZEATH

So peaceful and quiet in winter, empty houses stand silent and dark,
The shops are all gloomy. No customers here! No problem finding
somewhere to park.
The beach is deserted except for the gulls and maybe an odd
dog or two,
The clifftops are ours for solitary walks, and to soak up the
wonderful view.

Springtime arrives! The paintpots come out with the saws,
hammers and nails.
The traders perk up and start smiling again as they fill up the
shelves and the rails.
Here's summer at last! They all chortle with glee when the
visitors start to appear,
With their buckets and spades and surfboards galore,
they'll have a good time it is clear!
They buy wetsuits and boogies to ride the big waves,
fish and chips and pizzas to munch,
And as long as the sun shines from dawn until dusk, our tourists
are a real happy bunch

When autumn arrives and they've all gone home our batteries
we start to recharge.
'Have you had a good season?' Is the question most asked.
'Not too bad' we reply 'by and large.'

So it's back to square one, with no-one around.
Some like it some don't, you will find.
'Thank heavens they've gone.' say the wealthy retired
'The quietness we really don't mind.'

But when all's said and done, if the tourists don't come,
The shops will all close in Polzeath
Without visitors' money to keep open the doors,
The traders will all die a death.

So this is Polzeath, on the north Cornish coast,
You must take the good with the bad,
So the tourists go home in the right frame of mind
And say what a good time they've had.

*Valerie Cole*

## LIVING ON THE EDGE

I'm living on the edge
On the edge of what?
I'm walking on a tightrope
I'm feeling rather hot
Good morning Mrs Jones
It is a lovely day
The weather's fine
It's really warm
I think it's here to stay
Mrs Jones is lovely
She's really very kind
It truly is a marvellous world
It must be in the mind.

*Melvyn Roiter*

## LOVES SWEET ENIGMA

Come sit awhile mine love
Gaze into thine eyes
tell me what doth thou see?
'Tis reflections of thou love
entwined with thee.

Penetrate deeper
Searing through flesh and soul
Pray tell
what 'tis thy vision thou seek?

Beyond their misty darkness
Which doth fade
Shrouded mysteries
Unknown by any other

Spirit to spirit
Soul to soul
Truest love is never spake at all.

Reddest rose doth blossom
like unto thine hearts.
Rainbow colours are painted breath
panting
anticipating . . .

Taste of lover's sweetest wine
thou kiss which 'tis divine
Running red on lips and chins
from heaven's rarest vine.

*L J Povey*

## GOODBYE SWEET SOUL

Father as a little girl, I used to hold your hand.
Now I am clutching a red rose on a thorn.
You gave me the greatest gift of all.
Seeds of life.
I am leaving you in the garden of ever loving peace.
Where birds sing indifferently.
Trees bow their heads waiting for rain to hide their shame for ever
                                                    growing there.
Daffodils cry, roses sigh and bluebells borrow their colour from
                                                    the sky.

*Barbara Posner*

## BLIND DATE

They talked on the phone,
Then met on a bus.
She felt very alone.
He spoke about 'us'.

He was quite short and bald,
She was not much impressed.
'I'm so glad you called,'
He said with much zest.

'Whatever am I doing,'
She could hear herself say.
while he's busy wooing,
She should walk quickly away.

But after a time,
she quite liked him around.
He had said 'Be mine,'
True love, had she found?

Then came the punch line,
from out of the blue.
'My wife came to dine,
We are starting anew!'

No talks on the phone.
Nor rides on the bus.
She's really alone,
Because there's no 'us'!

*Susan Brooks*

## JANE

Look
At her
Ways
She smiles
And she
Says
Out of my
Life
I will not
Be your Wife
She smiles
And says
Look at my
Ways.

*Philip Allen*

# GHOSTLY FIGURE AROSE

he will go back
to Highgate cemetery that
one area to ask
so many other questions
how do they see him
when he goes on about
vampires and grisly things
he was arrested in
Highgate cemetery for a
disturbance or a breach
of the peace against
the place where some rest
the ghostly figure arose
so many years ago
ghost hunters were startled
what was the secret
of the one long mystery
even today it is unsolved
that place he got into
when it was shut up
why still question more
people of the same emotion
what can you get
not blood out of
some sorry old stone
so don't go back
the place draws you
right there again like
it is the simple reason
behind all evil thought

*Richard Clewlow*

## ILLICIT LOVE

We were married but not to each other
Yet we met. Was it purely by chance?
For neither of us were unhappy
But we fell deep in love with one glance
We both realised we were calling the tune
And the piper would find us one day
How would we feel when we settled the bill
What would he demand for his pay
Was it worth it this loving this hurting
For in this case the two were combined
There wasn't just two hearts to think of
Believe me our love was not blind
We agreed it all had to finish
We agreed only two hearts should break
We said our goodbyes nearly seven years ago
Someone tell me how long does it take?
How long does it take to forget love
Is it always as painful as this
Seven years - still I long for his warm hearted smile
For his smell, for his face, for his kiss
But life still goes on that's for certain
And the tale is all over - all told
There's only one thought I console myself with
Our love was not gilt 'twas pure gold.

*Jean Smith*

# THE SUN FROM THE MORNING MIST

Every ripened berry, every blade of grass twinkling with dew
bears witness from the morning mist, to a sun shining through
every lonely broken life saddened with the cry
searching for the reasons and the reasons why
put your trust in the saviour's love, he died for you
and like the sun from the morning mists, you will come shining through

*Ty Allbright*

## CREATION

Thank you Lord for families,
      The special people that we love,
May we value human beings,
      That are creative gifts from above.
Our God loves all the special friends,
      That we have been given.
Creative gifts from God above,
      The wonderful gift of human life.
The wonderful gift of love,
      The beautiful Earth below.
The beautiful Heavens above.

*Elizabeth De Meza*

## A Prayer

Oh God hold me in thy powerful hand
As I behold this wondrous land
Upon its beauty I look in awe
Knowing it would take many lifetimes more
To see the things thou hast placed on this earth for me
Oft times man forgets and reaps the merit
Forgetting you he takes all the credit
But has to realise at some given time
That he has stepped too far out of line
And, as he surveys the glorious earth
He has to admit that you gave it birth
And all things beneath and above in the sky
Belongs to you dear Lord who is seated on high

*M Hodges*

# THREADS OF LIFE
*(For my daughter Tracey)*

Gathering together the threads of life
Weaving them into dreams
Memories come flooding fast
Of things that might have been
Hurting each other causing so much pain
Unknown dreams and frightened tears
All that remains are thoughts of you
Only memories of what could have been
We were just too blind to see
What we could have done or what we could be

Haunting memories of a past that's now lost
Heartache, sorrow suffering life's cost
Dreams finally shattered to be laid aside
We cannot run we cannot hide
Always there embedded in our minds
The only hope left now, life's healer, time
The guilt, the pain the anger the shame
Never knowing who or what to blame
Sealed forever within the threads of life

To travel this road one can only hope
The chance to eventually pick up the threads
Of a past we both so terrifyingly dread
To share our sorrow and our grief
Handing over to time we must believe
Time unfolding will surely ease the pain
So we can gather the threads and face the world again.

**Graham Macnab**

## LIFE AND LIVING

We come into this world with nothing,
We can take nothing when we leave,
Our birth can make many happy,
Our dying can make many grieve,
We don't know how long we will be here,
On this earth where we must live each day.
We must make the most of our time spent,
Helping others along our life's way,
To build up many friendships,
We must take hold of many hands,
And we always should remember,
There are people in other lands,
To live in peace and harmony,
We must not go to war and fight,
We should try to listen, and understand,
And do what we think is right,
All these things are part of living,
And we must do the best we can,
To be loving as well as forgiving,
And have faith in our fellow man.

*Penny Rose*

## Ad-Lib

How many drops does it rain?
      (Voices distant)

How many colours in a field?
      (Images blurred)

How many shades has love?
      (Motions staggered)

How many sides has life?
      *(Textures rough)*

*G Parker*

## WENDY

I loved you before I ever met you
I held you before our hands did touch
I laid with you before I ever kissed you
I ached for you so very very much

I laughed with you before I ever knew you
I held you in my heart since I don't know when
I felt the warmth of you go coursing through me
I feel it so much stronger now than then

I've always known the joy that you would bring me
I've always walked with you through wind and rain
I've always dined with you by lighted candles
I've always, it seems always, known your name

I've laid with you on sun-kissed foreign beaches
I've held you naked in a sea of royal blue
I've watched you become the mother of our children
I've had the greatest dream I've ever had come true.

*R B May*

## I Wish I Could

I wish I could immerse
myself in a deep sea of
'nothing' -
'nothing' to do
'nothing' to say
'nothing' to think about
Just float and be at
peace and to rest.
This mood will pass, as other
moods do.
But 'nothing' will ever be the same.
My love has gone and left
me like this,
But, after a while I will surface,
And 'nothing' will become
'something' again.

*A M Moore*

## WHAT TO WEAR

My nephew's getting married
It will be a posh affair
I haven't got the invite yet
But wonder what I'll wear

I'll just look through my wardrobe
To see what dresses I can find
A turquoise silk with flowers
Is the one that springs to mind

Or what about my lilac suit
That may look rather pale
Although I have a hat to match
I once bought in a sale

I also have a green two-piece
I've only worn it twice
With just the right accessories
It could look really nice

On second thoughts I'll go to town
And buy me something new
I've found a lovely outfit
It's cream with navy blue

The wedding's getting nearer
I'm feeling quite excited
There's only one small problem
I've still not been invited

At last the postman brought it
He dropped it on the mat
My presence is requested
Now I'm off to buy the hat

I tried all shapes and sizes
Chose a cream one rather fancy
I'd like to think that on the day
I'll be the best dressed auntie.

*Barbara Welsby*

# WALKING THROUGH THE CEMETERY

As I was walking through the cemetery
On a lovely summer's day
I would feel my tears flowing down my face
Just coming to my mother's grave

I sat down beside her grave
Telling mum things I wanted her to know
Then I felt a cold breeze
I felt it was my mum talking to me

I felt I heard mum's voice
From above
Telling me she's in our Lord's care
I'm well and happy in his eternal home

I slowly walked from her grave
Wishing mum was with me today
My tears would flow for joy
Just having my mum.

*Janet Brown*

## UNTITLED

The earth is the Lord's I am his guest
His couch it is on which I rest.
His flock of birds sweet music trill
Upon my sunny windowsill.

His fields and hills my solace are
The morning dew the evening star
The fullness of the land and sea,
These precious gifts he trusts with me.

*Joyce M Waterfall*

## MORTALITY

Ae wee red rose-bud rears,
frae are cluster o'flours fast faded;
wee drafs o'dew, like tears
en jewels o'licht paraded.

Hud forever en memory's garden
tae temper thea passin' o'youth;
tae oor Creator, an' Earthly Warden
mortal fear o'thea ultimate truth.

*William Sinclair*

## Maybe

There are fairies at the bottom of my garden
they dance in a fairy ring,
If I listen very quietly I can hear them sing.
There are fairies at the bottom of my garden
a fairy king and queen,
There are fairies at the bottom of my garden,
Some folks say I'm silly others that I'm green,
There are fairies at the bottom of my garden
I know because I've seen.

*M Taylor*

# EASTENDERS

Eastenders is a programme
Which gets watched a lot
Actors are just brilliant
Everyone loves the plots
With the everyday happenings
You would want to join the cast
The programme is fantastic
You want to make it last.

*Lakshmi Agrawal*

# IN MY HEART

Buttercups of shimmering gold,
I'd like to keep in a treasure trove,
Silk and satin I would wear,
With sparkling diamonds twisted in my hair,
Unicorns of the purest white,
Would dance and make my days just right,
Hidden far away for me,
In a valley of peace and tranquillity,
The moon would strut across the sky,
Caressed by a thousand twinkling eyes,
And at the bottom of the sea,
A paint box of magical colours I'd keep,
Along the silvery shore I'd walk,
Collecting shells that seem to talk,
From the highest peak I'd see,
The whole world waiting for me,
Golden browns, pale greens, yellows and oranges,
Swaying trees,
Mother Nature's invisible thread,
Sewing together fields of red,
And in my heart I know it's true,
I need more than dreams to share with you,
I searched my mind,
I travelled the corridors of eternal youth,
A labyrinth of mystical spells,
I found doors I could not open,
And rooms of yesterday,
Then in my pocket I searched and found,
A happy memory of you all,
And in my heart I placed it,
To keep it safe and sound.

*D Cauch*

## SUNSET BAY

How beautiful it was
At the end of this day
To watch the golden sunset
Over the bay

The ships lie still
As dead as night
They will not sail
Till morning light

Waves come in
To wash the shore
Then out to sea
Back in once more

Out to sea
The ships will sail
Then the wind
Will blow a gentle gale.

*Adrian Newport*

## DESPAIR

He looks her up and down
His eyes filled with disgust
His jaw thrust out in anger

As the nauseous feeling deepens
Her body weakens
She hears every word before it's spoken

She's seen it a thousand times
She's ignored it a thousand times
She's never felt it, until now!

Her heart stops as she falls to the ground.

*Eilidh Scott*

## DREAM

I, had a dream, my love,
That we would meet again.
In some distance place
Where, there is no pain.

We would be young, and happy,
You were, my only true love
We would, never grow old,
Because we were so in love.

I, had a dream my love,
As we walked upon the clouds.
I told the world how I loved you
And shouted it out, to the crowds.

I awake from my dream, to find,
That we are old, and in pain.
We try to live each day anew,
To be thankful, and not complain.

No-one knows, how hard it is,
When your limbs are bent, and frail
But we always survive another day,
It's our love, that makes us prevail.

*K J Seeley*

## FOREVER FREE

Today there was a bird flying high
Across the deep blue ocean
Without a question why.
A distance between us but no distance apart.
No reason to end and no reason to start.
Gathering food for its travels
And harmony for its heart.
This bird was a soul with knowledge,
Knowing where to go.
A passion for a journey to lead
it where a waterfall can
only flow.

*Gary James Taylor*

# I Was A Stranger In A Strange Land

Weaned from my comfort,
My safeness; I stand alone,
Alien fields stretch out
Foreign to me; I am alone!

The sounds I hear of streams
Through valley and ravines,
Have common familiar noise meseems,
But dark circling Cimmerian Milvines

Squawk their threats that
Carry to my ears, as hidden
hunters of my life's blood that,
Sprinkled widely on foreign ground forbidden,

I long for the safety of my mother's breast,
The cold marble pillow
for my head to rest,
Alone, lonely am I as a widow,

I wander, as a Hebrew,
No land is mine, But all!
Thy kingdom; the being in me withdrew,
I stand before the mighty Yew,

Infinitesimal!

*Bruce Allen*

# A DIAMOND IS FOREVER

A diamond is forever
shining in her sky.
The moon had
crossed city streets
to be close by.
To be with you tonight,
there's a tear in
my eye.
Outside your window
Young lovers
Quietly passing by.
A diamond is forever
Just hanging in
the sky.

*K Lake*

## THE END OF THE AGE!

I look back remember
  Our nation that was
Greatest of Empires ever
  of Christians because

Our servants faithfully
  Carried out that fine task
Upholding the faith
  Of our forefathers passed

For God King and country
  Men fought to the last
Defending our shores
  From invaders great blast

Of bombs rockets galore
  millions lost lives to defeat
The rights of our Britain
  Until final end treat.

We look back in anger
  of all we see raw
Our proud Union Jack
  And mad English law!

The devil, age here
  As our Lord rightly said
Before end of age -
  To nation, death we are lead!

*Geoffrey Wilyman*

## THE HAPPY DAYS

The happy days are the ones
we remember so well, the
unhappy days are those that
we try to forget for they
only ever bring sadness
and tears.

*Michael Spittles*

## THE MEETING OF THE CLAN

Now I have reached the age of eighty-two
There is one thing I have wanted to do
It is to get all my grandchildren in a queue
I have ten great grandchildren and ten grandchildren too

My pension money does not go far
So I will have to see what I can spare
I would like to treat them when I can
This would make me happy as head of the clan

I do not drink and I do not smoke
That makes some think I am a queer bloke
But I am not that bad I am a caring man
I am glad to be head of the clan.

*William Howarth*

## WHAT LIFE

What life is this I live?
I have no time to give to those I love.
Instead, I pledge my all to those who pay
                      my daily bread.

They take my strength, my skill, my mind.
They leave me scratching 'mongst the debris
                        left behind
for something of myself that I can leave
to those I will to live beyond my grave:

That they might say. We are the richer
                   for that he gave.

*Jesse Walton*

## SUNRISE AMONG THE CUMBRIAN MOUNTAINS

As fire, in mists,
The kindled mountains, before dawn,
All roar like lions,
And raise their fierce beaks, glowing,
To shake their cliffy manes
In orange-pointed flames . . .

Below, the dales so green
That slumbers like the sea -
Where mists like a river run, and where the streams
Like little cloudlets play,
Hang from the crags, and waft
Between pure beams,
And lift away like birds, while ecstasy
Shoots under me like wings
- My world, while divine beings look on!

You deer and foxes, you scattered flocks and small black cattle herds
And forests shadowing;
You river-brows, like skylarks, wake and soar
While peregrine, buzzard, eagle, hover and stoop easily! . . .

Now, look; how light, so liquid-white, sharp, bright as knives,
Whets out of space around;
Breaks into every rock and sod
And, bursting, blistering, blinding it,
Irradiates the thundering world . . .

My land!

*Wilfrid Leng*

## WARTIME MEMORIES

'Twas in the year of
forty-three
And World War Two was
at its height,
Young sailors, soldiers and
airmen
Joining in the fight
Dead and dying all
around
Bombs scattered along
the ground
Young and old running here
and there, all confused
'And deep despair.'

Among the dead and dying
A young soldier boy kept sighing,
my life is fading fast my friends
And I'm not coming home
You will all go back to England
And I will be here alone.
So bury me deep on the hillside
Under the rising sun
Wrapped in the flag
I fought for
My duty for England
is done.

*A K Guest*

# DAVID

He emerged from the crowd, this boy, this youth, soon to be a man.
His left leg, heavy, dragging, his arm hanging useless, limp.
Distorted features, twisted smile, but a bright light shone.
He stood, alone, in the crowd, dignified in his isolation

She, seeing him, paused, this boy, so like her son.
Was drawn to him, not by pity or compassion, but by love.
He shone, this boy, a bright light on a dark and sombre day.
The feeling drew her closer and they began to speak.

She felt no urge to help as he struggled with his words,
Each one draining his strength in its utterance.
The effort only served to make him more courageous in her eyes
She had watched her own son struggle in this way.

Seen him fight and be conqueror in the end.
Slowly, slowly, the story was told and still the bright light shone.
A balcony high, a fall, a scream, a life despoiled
A body crippled, but not a crippled soul, the light still shone.

His humour, love and courage enfolded her
She asked his name, need not have done, by now she knew.
He smiled. 'David' he said, 'David is my name,'
Her son too bears that name, and this boy so like her own.

In courage and in spirit, will remain with her, inside her heart.
A spark, a jewel, to lighten up the darkest days
She knew him for so short a time, this other David
This small spark, which could light the world
As it lit her life.

*C M Bellamy*

# MIND OR MAN, CONSCIENCE OR HONOUR

A lack of bravery and excess of words,
Did lead to a job unfinished.
The man who swore upon the ghost,
Through thought let his passion diminish.
His task though not easy was clear,
And when moved by the dream of an actor,
He for his cause could not shed a tear.
Through discourse of reason he did question,
The undefinable plight of man.
But apart from condemn himself,
This did little but delay his great plan.
And perhaps suggest that Hamlet is more mind than man.

*Andrew Waters*

## LIFE

I feel like I'm a flower,
Blowing in the breeze.
My stalk starts to break
To make me fall down on my knees.
I remember days were happy,
And minutes coloured gold.
But the colour starts to fade,
And my heart is getting cold.
Now my grip on life is slipping,
As my hand begins to frail
So life isn't coloured gold,
The colour has gone pale.
All at once I'm in a box,
On my way to God,
I wonder what will lie ahead
As I cry beneath the sod.

*Andrea Hayes*

# LIFE AND I

Life and I are like lovers, straying
Amid the happy throng
And often like young children playing
So full of fun and song

Life plucks all the blooming hours
That grow fast day by day
Pressing on my brow like flowers
Sometimes I feel like the Queen of May

Then once again in rainy weather
As we sit side by side
Planning what we'll do together
In the coming years we have to bide

Sometimes life denies me blisses
Then I may frown or pout
But, we can make up with kisses
Before the day is out

Then he always grows more zealous
Tender, and ever more so true
Love's the more for being jealous
Just as all true lovers do.

*Mary Elizabeth Bridges*

## A NEW DAY

As night time quietly drifts away
The sun comes up to start a new day
The air is fresh with dew on the grass
With energy you hope will last
To do many things you have planned
On this summer day that is so grand
Quickly doing the usual chores
Thinking this is such a bore
Sunshine beckons you go outside
Your face lights up with a smile
Sitting relaxed under blue skies
With soft white clouds passing by
Colourful flowers in full bloom
This moment is precious and new
The sights of nature do astound
With fragrance and lovely sounds
To make the most of warm sunshine
There is no better way to pass the time
Long forgotten are those chores
It's far too nice to stay indoors.

*Pauline Ann Ibrahim*

# LOVE IS ...

Love is the spark, that lights up the dark
It's the seed of all Creation.
Love is the key, that sets life free
Happiness, its destination.

Love is the Hope, when you feel you can't cope
With life and its frustration.
Love is in me, endlessly
Love is my inspiration.

Love is rare and sometimes unfair,
Broken hearts and devastation
but love lives on, like that classic song
Despite the fear, the complication.

Love is a drug, it gets in the blood,
to the soul it's infestation.
Love is the cure, to all that's impure
Love is a fascination.

Love can disguise, it's so full of surprise.
Love lives with anticipation.
Love is a power, delicate as a flower
Love feeds the imagination.

Love is the plea, so emotionally
To the hate filled dying nation.
If only we'd see how great love can be
and live as one in unification.

*Michael McArdle*

# HOPE ON THE FOURTH OF JULY

*This poem is dedicated to Nicola, in loving memory of baby Hope,*
*(miscarried on July 4th1997)*

Hope is your given name
And that is what you have given in return,
You brought both pain and joy
Rest in peace we both yearn.

Born on the fourth of July
But only to die,
Rest in peace we both yearn.

Every year we will remember you
In our thoughts and things we do,
Rest in peace our little babe
Wrapped in the thoughts that we will always
Be loving you.

***Mark Milton***

# COLOURS OF NATURE

Green is the colour that I seek and with it form my bonds
Because my eyes they feel caressed and soothed by verdant fronds
I roam in forests deep and dark but never feeling gloom
For I'm in the emerald heart of nature's ever-giving womb.

Blue is the oceans and skies and plays its own conquest
To ride on rolling fluent seas, to rise from wave to crest
The earth is draped in sapphire gowns and dressed to love and lure
From its darkest turquoise depths to the sweetened sky's azure

White is the true light, that is pure, sure, a certainty
Like cascading, tumbling mountain rivers reach the sea
And melting snow-crowned mountains feed the waters that they take
Their foaming torrents sweep the smoothened boulders in their wake

Black is the darkness like the great abyssal depths of night
But even then the void is pierced with pinpoint specks of light
But not when lurking clouds obscure the starlight's sharp detail
Below the land lies tainted black beneath their raven veil.

Yellow is the blazing sun whose rays touch earth with life
And the soft fluorescent moon becomes the night-time's wife
They work their topaz shifts to earn a living for the globe
And so the world's forever clad in nature's golden robe

Red is that time of evening when the clouds put on their show
Illuminated by the setting sun's last ruby glow,
But also orange, pink and lilac add to their prism charms
And so I feel embraced by nature's multi-coloured arms
And my heart spills open as her psychedelic hand
Bows down to cast a goodnight kiss upon the faded land.

*Eddy Shanks*

## THE DISSERTATION

Gathering material for my dissertation,
seeking evidence of William Morris.
Visiting churches in anticipation,
Throughout Staffordshire for my thesis.

First to Leek, rich in embroidery,
To Wardles, art of dyeing.
St Edward's windows, exemplary.
William's hands, blue with blueing.

The Tursar silk, vegetable dyed.
Produced altar cloths and vestments.
Found in numerous churches, with pride.
Distinctive styles of Morris's achievements.

One of the finest churches in Britain,
so said Betjeman, of All Saints.
No wonder he was so smitten,
with sights, and no restraints.

Burne Jones' windows, oh so fine.
Needlework depicting angels.
Shaw's altar frontals, so divine.
Walls and ceilings, relating to the gospels.

Moorland village churches,
Keys available, at the vicarage.
Reveals all, to the researchers.
Decorative windows, thick in foliage.

He came to Leek, to learn to dye,
A prodigious man indeed.
Fabrics and wallpapers, to please the eye.
The legacy of Morris, to succeed.

*Raymond Baggaley*

## MY THOUGHTS

Cleaning the car, polishing the windows,
Walking the dog, hanging out the washing,
I pause.
I think of you.
Queuing in the supermarket, cooking the tea,
Bathing the baby, making the beds,
I pause.
I think of you.

Sitting in the sunshine looking at the sea,
Children playing quite oblivious to
My pause.
No more the song birds, no more the joys of life,
No more the moon and the stars.
No more suffering.
Just peace.

*Yvonne Jordan*

## SURROUNDED BY A WALL

Inside I sit behind a wall,
Which stretches above me - oh so tall,
It hides my feelings of hurt and pain,
But gives no hope nor reasons for gain.

Outside the people stand and stare,
But life's like that - so unfair.

The pain inside cannot be seen,
For no smile is visible beyond my screen.

My unhappiness is shown by a glistening tear,
Which reveals the hidden hurt and fear.

So behind this wall I shall remain,
To helplessly fight my mind in pain.

I'll never give in - *I shall succeed*
My will to live is far from greed,
The sparkle of hope is like a seed,
The help of others is all that I need.

***Tracey Wheeler***

# LOVE

Like bright pink balloons
Floating high above
Joyful, colourful
that's the feeling of love.
Like bubbles colliding
then going pop.
Praying to God
that it never will stop.
Beacons of light
as they go on their way
A love that shines
is here to stay
Lifting the spirits
of young and old
Light as air feelings
More precious than gold.

*R Kelly*

## STOP MAKING WAR AND WORK AT PEACE

So much fighting and so many wars,
So much energy on them spent . . .
Causing pain and so many scars,
So much grieving this has meant.
It once was said 'War could end War',
Since then there's been so little peace.
Love needs to rule forever more,
Soon making violence cease.
Man's inhumanity to man,
Brings extra suffering to our lives,
Learning to love more should mean we can,
Live in peace while everyone strives,
To live out a new moral code,
Making the world a better place,
By our living in peaceful mode.
Filling life with divine grace.
We should change our lives with all speed
By turning to more loving style,
Sadly if we ignore, not heed,
Our lives won't prove to be worthwhile.
Failing the change, our world will slide,
At an ever-increasing pace,
Crime and violence, genocide,
Will destroy all the human race.
Each one of us should stop and think
And bring about much needed change,
Then our actions could make a link,
Love and peace through our lives could range.

***Ruby Lawrence***

# A SENSE OF BELONGING

We all need a sense of
belonging. These days, for
security reasons, as well
as a peace of mind, against
the wild outback world.

The more common need
is the family unit, to which
all mankind belong, which
gives one fruits of peace, love and joy -

Which all people long for, and
few attain, in this world.
Gifts which money or property
cannot buy.

For those who chose to remain
loyal to one's family.
Peace of mind, joy of heart
and every happiness will always
be theirs.

Such love and happiness
will grow as one's family
grows up.

*Norman Mason*

## A REQUEST FOR A POEM
*(In dedication to Sylvia, my wife, my life)*

Composing just twenty lines, I find that shirty
Because I usually like to do thirty
But I'll put my skill to work
I never was one to shirk
It seems too short to express a view
Well for me, but I don't know about you.
Not enough words to just relate
Neither even to contemplate
Many poems I've written, some good
Others portray like a lump of wood
I've composed for magazines, friends as well
When they get published I feel swell
Forty seven so far that can't be bad
Royalties coming in of that I'm glad
Words to flow and to rhyme
It's that, that takes the time
But I enjoy this way of life
Although it causes me a lot of strife
Finished at last, now start again
More paper more work and more pain.

***Prince Rhan of Kathari***

# MY FRIEND!

Only known you for over a year
On my face I feel a tear
Kind, affectionate strong and loving
How I wish you weren't going
Taught me things I never knew
As my friend I'll remember you
As your friend don't forget me please
As it feels you're going overseas
I pray you succeed there as you did here
Still, mustn't worry as you're still quite near
Christmas and birthdays are when I show care
Through gifts and hugs, I want to share
You're one of God's people, I love so dearly
In my mind I see you clearly
Knowing you was such a privilege
Last days with you at Bradwell
Pilgrimage
*God bless you my friend.*

**Joanne Stephens**

# THE BIRTHDAY PARTY

It's Carol's birthday and excitement fills the air,
The table to lay, food to prepare.
Jelly, blancmange, cakes galore,
Ice-cream, biscuits and so much more.
Everyone arrives in their finest clothes,
Presents wrapped with pretty bows.
'What shall we play?' a child declares,
'I know' said one 'musical chairs.'
The music goes with a joyous sound,
Jostling and dancing all around.
Blind man's buff is always fun,
See the children scream and run.

'Come on children, time to eat.
Settle down, have a treat.'
The birthday cake takes pride of place,
A look of joy on each one's face.
Sticky fingers, sticky thumbs,
Lots of mess, loads of crumbs.
'Now,' says mother 'before you go,
We're going to have a puppet show,'
Dancing dolls, wooden clowns,
Jumping moving, up and down.
They all look on in sheer delight,
At the colourful scene, 'what a sight'.
The atmosphere is filled with joy,
Fun for every girl and boy.
'Blow out the candles, let us cheer,
*Happy birthday, happy year!'*

**Wendy Watkin**

# FRIENDSHIP

Friendship's ingredients feed the spirit
On acceptance comes the meaning of it
Brings with it no uncertainty
Long or short it's for permanency.

Eager to share happiness sadness good and bad
Telling of quality and value makes one glad
Constant always in word and deed
Helpful this is when one is in need.

Steps for taking could add to pleasure
Filling the cup to full measure
Prize of friendship for the young or old
To each this comes more precious than gold.

Those in search of this treasure
It's theirs to have in full measure
Shorten the distance for making a friend
Together through life your way to wend.

*Hannah Birch*

## THE CHANGING SEASON

Smoke spiralling lazily upwards
Drifts from the smouldering fire.
Dried leaves, swept by the wind
Into ever-changing patterns.

Gardens denuded of bright colours
Show the muted shades
Of orange, yellow and gold.
Leaves turning to russet.

The sun low in the sky
A crimson pool
Dips below the horizon
And everywhere the scent of autumn.

*Julie Hazel Kyme*

## THE ICE MAIDEN

500 years in an
ancient tomb,
the Ice Maiden laid
in sacrificed gloom.

Wrapped in fine garments
of colourful wool,
her long straight
dark hair,
her eyes empty
pools.

A volcanic explosion
tore open her grave,
spilling its contents
into the sun's blaze.

Her features are
dried,
although people still
try, to find out her
past and what
secrets she hides . . .

*Penny Verney*

## MARRIED LIFE

Round town tonight for your final fling
Oh no, not the karaoke, no-one can sing
Before married life.

Next Saturday night you'll no longer be a spinster
I thought you'd be getting married in York Minster
What's married life?

No regrets now it's too late for that
Have you really got your Dad to wear that daft hat?
Help! Married life.

When you've said your vows and the bells go dong
You'll still have to rush home to see your cat Tom
Here's to married life.

When you've ate all your chicken at the reception
The speeches will start, here comes the deception
This is married life.

When your tongue's dropped off through talking to your relations
You feel elation over the whole occasion
It's married life.

Off to France now with your trailer tent
A stove, two sleeping bags that your Mum and Dad lent
'Just married' life.

When you return you're still on honeymoon
Until while down the pub he gets drunk with the rugby team
                                            from Troon
Oh no! Married life.

Have you thought about what happens when the kids come along
The tears, the laughter, the memories of when you were young
Long and happy married life.

*Sylvia J King*

## HUNGER

Let my hunger consume me.
Days without breakfast, lunch or tea,
Will bring at first happiness,
Followed by exercises and restlessness.
Not to forget the bouts of depression.
Diet Cokes will be the only drinking session,
The weighing scales will show what it's all for,
The mirror cannot be relied on for the score,
No matter what, more weight shall be lost,
Ignore the depression, carry on at every cost,
And in time, Diet will not be my second name,
I shall win this fight or face shame.
Throw all food given to one away,
Because if eaten, I lose more than a day.
I'm aware of extreme cold in warm weather,
So wear lots of clothes altogether.
Sleepless nights may be long,
But it doesn't mean anything is wrong.
I keep busy for as long as I can,
Then it's easier to keep on a food ban.
Hunger will never trouble me anymore,
It makes me feel clean to my inner core.
I'll keep on, no matter what,
Even though I'll feel the cold more than the hot.
Remember that I'm fatter than I dare admit,
Soon, all of my jeans will fit.
Take no notice of what people say,
It's what I don't eat that matters at the close of day.
So, soon I'll be on the road to fitness and health,
In the long run perhaps it's better than wealth.
I won't start tomorrow, but today,
It's all that I have got left, it's the only way.

*C I Parker*

## ALL THINGS RIGHT

God is a good God,
For He puts all things right,
We work for Him all the time.

Look unto Jesus, for He is the Father in our lives,
He is the King of kings and the Lord of lords,
We give Him all the glory, for ever and ever,
He is the King of love, and is great
In the eyes of His people.

We'll kneel at the feet of Jesus
In Him we will sing to the Lord,
In joy, for He loves us all.

*K L C Green*

# ME

I said 'Goodbye' to a
person called 'Me',
I didn't like her
Very much you see.

I got so confused and lost
along the way,
Listening to what others
would say.

Trying to make me into
something I'm not.
I just wanted to be loved
'For me',
'For me' is all I've got!

I longed to become someone
'New'
Hoping you would love her too.

Why did I let that other
person go?
That person was really
'Me'
now I know!

*Janet 'Rose' Marsh*

## EMOTIONAL HIGHS AND LOWS

Listen, news to share,
One's met someone special, lots to tell
Such a happy event it's rung love's bell
Encounter to spread many must know
Hours spent on phone calls
Emotions in, then out of control
If all happens to fall flat
Envy creeps in
Jealousy silently cries
Emotions return to lows from highs.

*Alan Jones*

# INFORMATION

We hope you have enjoyed reading this book - and that you will continue to enjoy it in the coming years.

If you like reading and writing poetry drop us a line, or give us a call, and we'll send you a free information pack.

Write to :-
**Anchor Books Information**
**1-2 Wainman Road**
**Woodston**
**Peterborough**
**PE2 7BU**
**(01733) 230761**